PSYCHOLOGY
AND
RETROCAUSALITY

HOW THE FUTURE DETERMINES
LOVE, MEMORY, EVOLUTION,
LEARNING, DEPRESSION, DEATH,
AND WHAT IT MEANS TO BE HUMAN

MARK HATALA, PH.D.

GREENTOP ACADEMIC PRESS ✦ GREENTOP, MISSOURI

Psychology and retrocausality: How the future determines love, memory, evolution, learning, depression, death, and what it means to be human
by Mark Hatala, Ph.D.

ISBN-13: 978-1-933167-57-2
ISBN-10: 1-933167-57-2

Book Design: Charles Dunbar

Table of Contents

Preface

It seems unlikely that you would have picked up this book without knowing what retrocausality is, but it can be understood simply as the future impacting (or determining) the present and the past. We generally live in a world of unilateral causality, where the past determines the present and the future. Retrocausality argues the opposite.

This is not to say that everything in life is determined retrocausally, but rather that it is an underappreciated and usually unacknowledged explanatory factor. The purpose of this series of essays is to show how a number of different psychological phenomena can be explained through retrocausality. I'm not presenting any original research of my own, but rather reinterpreting the findings of others to show how they have a retrocausal explanation. This is similar to the work of Edwin Ray Guthrie, a behaviorist in the 1930s, who used the research of other psychologists to prove that his theory of learning was correct. It's all a matter of perspective and reinterpreting results in a different way.

I want to take a moment to discuss what this book is *not* about. It's not about psi, paranormal activity, ESP, clairvoyance, or prophesy. Although there is pseudoscientific "research" on all of those topics, they are about predicting the future rather than showing how the future determines the present and past. I have also left out the work on precognitive dreaming. It may be true that Abraham Lincoln dreamed of his own death for the three nights preceding his assassination or that Mark Twain dreamed of his brother's death in a steamboat accident days before it happened, but I believe that dream interpretation is, at best, problematic, and should be left to others. While some researchers claim that precognitive dreaming is the strongest proof of the existence of psi, I believe that is the equivalent of being the best-looking child in an incredibly ugly family.

Thanks for reading this book.

Mark Hatala, Ph.D.
Professor of Psychology
Truman State University

Memory

The place to start any discussion of psychology and retrocausality is with the topic of memory, because the ability to remember the past or think about the future underlies both what it means to be human and how the future impacts the present. The problem with memory is that we can only remember things that have already happened. Unless, of course, you live life "backwards." Lewis Carroll made a point of this in *Through the Looking Glass and What Alice Found There* through a conversation between Alice and the White Queen:

> "I don't understand you," said Alice. "It's dreadfully confusing!"
> "That's the effect of living backwards," the Queen said kindly:
> "It always makes one a little giddy at first - - "
> "Living backwards!" Alice repeated in great astonishment. "I
> never heard of such a thing!"
> "- - but there's one great advantage in it, that one's memory
> works both ways."
> "I'm sure MINE only works one way," Alice remarked.
> "I can't remember things before they happen."
> "It's a poor sort of memory that only works backwards,"
> the Queen remarked.

In a nutshell, this is what retrocausality is about - remembering the future. Getting memory to "work both ways." Not surprisingly, the musings of Lewis Carroll are not accounted for in the Atkinson-Shiffrin model of memory, a model so dominant in psychology that it is referred to as the "modal model" of memory. The Atkinson-Shiffrin model proposes three storage systems, each with their own capacity and duration limits. Sensory memory (sometimes called the *sensory register*) stores all incoming information we are aware of for a very brief period of time, usually less than half a second. This feeds into short-term memory (sometimes called *working memory*) which holds seven or so "chunks" of information active for approximately thirty seconds. Short-term memory can be thought of as what we are consciously aware of at any moment. Long-term memory, on the other hand, has no capacity limits, and depending on your religious beliefs, the duration is eternal. The problem with long-term memory is in accessing the information, an acute issue for anyone who has lost their keys. The focus of retrocausality research is on long-term memory, and there have been intriguing findings.

The study which put the concept of retrocausality into the subject matter of psychology is Daniel Bem's "Feeling the Future" studies from 2011, published in the premier, peer-reviewed *Journal of Personality and Social Psychology*. Publishing the research was so controversial that the editors of *JPSP* felt compelled to write a brief explanation of why they had chosen to publish the article at all. What had Bem found? Experimental evidence for anomalous retroactive influences on cognition and affect, as the full title of his article explains. But what does that mean?

Bem performed a series of nine studies which showed evidence of retrocausal knowledge in college students. For example, in one study, students were told that they would see pictures of two curtains, one of which had a picture behind it. They were to pick the curtain that they believed hid the picture. They were told that some of the pictures were of "explicit erotic images," which were couples having nonviolent (but explicit) sex. Participants were also given the option of seeing male-male or female-female erotic images, so that everyone was happy. Non-erotic pictures were of couples kissing or posing, but were not particularly sexual. The participants were exposed to 36 trials, and in each trial had a 50/50 chance of picking the curtain with a picture behind it. The sequencing of the curtains (picture on the left or right) and pictures (erotic or non-erotic) was random.

Bem found that people were able to identify where the erotic pictures would be 53.1% of the time, which is statistically greater than chance. For the non-erotic pictures, the correct "hit rate" was 49.8%, which is no different from chance. Bem discounted the possibility of the study results coming from clairvoyance (sometimes referred to as *remote viewing*) because the information on which curtain the image would appear behind was not "stored" in the computer somewhere, but randomly determined *after* the participant had made their choice of a curtain. Similarly, he dismissed the possibility of psychokinesis, which would argue that the participant psychically influenced where the image would appear, due to the way the randomization of images occurred. Instead, Bem attributed the results to retroactive influence based on the idea that throughout evolutionary history, a survival and reproductive advantage would come from correctly anticipating sexual stimuli. Therefore, people are able to "feel the future" in order to be exposed to erotic pictures.

A second example from this series of studies would be helpful to clarify the retrocausal impact on memory, and it comes directly from the conversation Alice has with the White Queen. It is an established finding in memory research that *rehearsal* (or repeating) of information leads to better recall of that same information. This is how and why people study for an exam - to put the "to-be-remembered" course information into long-term memory for later recall during the exam. But what if you study the exam material *after* the exam? Would you be able to "live backwards?"

The "White Queen" study had participants sit in front of a computer where they were presented with 48 concrete nouns (like *cat*) which were drawn from four categories (animals, foods, clothes, and occupations). Each word was presented for three seconds, and the participant was told to try to create a visual image of the word, so if they saw the word *cow*, they should think about a cow eating grass in a field or being milked. They were then given a surprise free recall task, where they were asked to type out as many of the 48 words as they could remember. They were then given a post-recall task where 24 words from the previous list (six from each of the four categories) were randomly presented and the participant was asked to click on each word in a particular category (which would then turn red), and then type the word out. The 24 words were then rescrabled and the task was repeated for each of the other categories.

The results of the study were surprising, but consistent with a retrocausal explanation of memory. Bem found that the 24 words randomly presented in the post-recall task were significantly more likely to have been remembered in the earlier free recall task. In other words, the classifying and typing task which they performed in the future directly impacted their free recall of words in the past. The participants were rehearsing in the future information which they had recalled in the past. They were "thinking backwards!" This clearly violates a unilinear view of causality and suggests that the White Queen was correct.

Was Bem celebrated for having achieved a scientific breakthrough? Hardly! His results were dismissed immediately by researchers who claimed that the studies couldn't be replicated. My favorite criticism was that Bem's results "do not represent reality." He was also criticized for his experimental design and statistical analysis, although the journal editors and reviewers had gone through them with a fine-toothed comb - they realized the blowback that would be caused by publishing the article (perhaps further confirmatory evidence of retrocausality?). So how did Bem get the results that he found? Luck, questionable research practices, "generous rounding" of numbers, selective data reporting, and "hypothesizing after results are known" (called *HARKing*) were all offered as possible explanations. The scientific outrage was so furious that research of this type has effectively ceased.

I believe that part of the blowback problem lies with Daniel Bem himself. All scientific research is presented within a theoretical structure, and the structure he chose for this series of studies was that of *psi*. What is psi? It's mostly a more scientific term for ESP or "extrasensory perception," and is something of a catch-all category of unexplainable phenomena. Psi includes things like *telepathy* (where information is passed from one individual to another mentally), *premonition* (when you just know something awful is going to happen), and *prophesy*. It attracts people who are very much into prospective dream analysis and past life regression. In other words, grifters, swindlers, and con artists. But not scientists.

I believe another major mistake was in his use (or lack of use) of the participants. Sensitivity to retrocausal knowledge might be normally distributed throughout the population in a bell curve, in much the same way as height, weight, and intelligence. Instead of using different people in each of his nine studies, he should have identified the participants who did the "best" or showed the most evidence of retrocausal sensitivity, and used them as the participants in *all* of the studies. After all, if you want to appraise how good a wine is, you don't bring in people off the street, you call in the experts! By limiting his subject pool and focusing his research on participants who showed evidence of retrocausal identification (with the curtains) and recall (with the words), Bem's results would have been even more significant.

However, I believe the biggest problem with Bem's research is that none of the experiments were personally meaningful for the participants. While they were given extra credit in a psychology course or $5 for their participation, the activities they completed had no bearing on their life experience. Pick which curtain has a picture behind it. Read some words and recall them. These are tasks which have no meaning or consequences for the participants. Not like the crucial life events which we discuss in the rest of this book. Love, luck, learning, mental health, intelligence, and death have an enormous impact on our individual lives. And memory underlies them all.

This is because memory, properly understood, is retrocausal.

Love

Is there a science to falling in love? A series of steps that one can follow to ensure love happens? Apparently, it depends on your perspective. In 1995, Ellen Fein and Sherrie Schneider had a best-seller with *The Rules: Time-Tested Secrets for Capturing the Heart of Mr. Right*. The first rule was to "Be a Creature Unlike Any Other," which seems straightforward enough. At least you don't have to be someone else. After all, Oscar Wilde said to "Be yourself. Everyone else is already taken."

Has dating changed in the last 25 years since *The Rules* was published? Of course not! *The Rules* was never about falling in love, it was about finding a partner and getting married. Similarly, the "male" equivalent book, *The Game: Penetrating the Secret Society of Pickup Artists* by Neil Strauss, wasn't about "love" either, although it presented plenty of advice about *sarging* (engaging in conversation to seduce a woman).

I teach classes on cognitive science as well as romantic relationships. A comment I often get in my cognitive science class goes something like, "I've read three books on cognitive science, and I still have no idea what it is." My response to this is "Exactly!" Substitute the word "love" for "cognitive science" and the same could be said for the students in my romantic relationships class, although that's not completely true. Although they realize that research into matters of the heart is inconclusive, they still know what "love" in their own life looks like.

I propose that a particular type of love, what is commonly referred to as "love at first sight" is actually a retrocausal phenomenon. Sometimes you just *know* that someone is the right person for you for the rest of your life the first time you meet. As a woman in *When Harry Met Sally* says about the moment her future husband walked across the room to introduce himself to her, "At that moment I knew. I knew the way you know about a good melon."

The idea of love at first sight has a long past, but a short history. It appears to be mutual in the Bible (Genesis 24) when Issac and Rebekah meet for the first time. When Rebekah sees Issac walking towards her, it is described as "And Rebekah lifted up her eyes, and when she saw Issac, she lighted off the camel. For she had said unto the servant, What man is this that walketh in the field to meet us?" (Genesis 24:64-65, KJV). Issac makes her his wife then and there. Their son Jacob has a similar experience when he first encounters Rachel watering her father's sheep by a well - "And Jacob kissed Rachel, and lifted up his voice, and wept" (Genesis 29:11, KJV).

The ancient Greeks and Romans had a similar idea of people (usually men) who were overcome by a type of passionate madness (*theia mania* - "madness from the gods") caused by their heart being shot through with "love's arrows" fired by Cupid. This image has stayed with Western culture through Renaissance art to the Valentine's Day cards of our present time.

But is there any psychological research to support the idea of an instant, passionate attraction that leads to long lasting love? Of course there is! Some researchers believe that it all comes down to physical attractiveness. People can judge the attractiveness of someone they meet in less than a second, and attractive people are nine times more likely to have people fall in love with them instantly. Another mitigating factor is perceived trustworthiness. True or not, people believe that they can look into the eyes of a stranger and determine how trustworthy they are. Put those two factors together, and you explain the phenomena, especially since love at first sight isn't often a *shared* experience. Men are much more likely to report the experience than women, and this has been attributed to the fact that men are more likely to judge partners based on perceived physical attractiveness.

Researchers have also investigated whether the love at first sight phenomena is a retrospective memory effect. All couples reminisce about how they met, and how they initially felt about their partner. Do people "change their story" to make things seem foreordained? That does NOT seem to be the norm. While couples may bicker about who fell in love faster or "deeper," they don't create illusions about their initial feelings. Men and women who fall in love instantly readily admit it early in the relationship, and don't feel the need to change the romantic narrative later.

To put the phenomenon in a theoretical context, the current dominant theory of love is Sternberg's proposal that love has three components: passion, commitment, and intimacy. Many relationships are able to achieve two of these components. For example, passion and commitment lead to short-lived Vegas weddings, passion and intimacy are indicative of "summer flings" among the young, and commitment and intimacy are the components of couples who reach their 50s and 60s (and older). By that point, they're not hopping into bed every night ready to burn up the sheets. When a relationship is able to achieve all three components, Sternberg calls that "consummate love," and that is the life-long partner relationship that everyone aspires to achieve.

This has led to the consensus view among researchers that by Sternberg's criteria, love at first sight isn't really "love" at all, but rather a strong initial attraction marked by excitement and exhilaration. And yet, 55%

of people who say they experienced love at first sight married the person who caused it! It might be helpful to study THEIR experience before drawing conclusions about everyone else. Something else is clearly going on here, and I propose that it has a retrocausal explanation.

Here are some of the commonalities associated with relationships that begin with love at first sight and culminate in consummate love. First, they felt "butterflies" in their stomach, indicating a visceral "gut" reaction on meeting the love of their life. They literally "knew in their bones" that this was the right person for them. Second, they remember the eye contact. There is a sensation that this person is the only person they see in an otherwise crowded room. And that person is fascinating, which leads to the third point - the initial conversation goes far beyond "small talk" and they want to know everything about the other person, not as if they were a stranger, but as if they have been separated for some time. Finally, they had a sense of familiarity with the other person which some have described as a "paradoxical feeling of not knowing and instantly knowing" the other person completely. I propose that what they're feeling is a shared future which they have not yet experienced together, but can't wait to begin.

While I'm tempted to end this topic with a rehash of the blind date where Prince Harry met and instantly fell in love with Meghan Markle, instead I want to finish with a personal example. My brother met his wife in kindergarten, instantly fell in love with her, and asked her to marry him. Of course she rejected his proposal - who gets married at age five? She added the extra sting of saying that she didn't want to marry a "stinkpot" (her words, not mine). They remained close friends until she moved away in fifth grade. As this was the pre-Facebook 1970s, although she moved to another suburb 10 miles away, they lost all contact with each other. My brother had no girlfriends in high school, and lived at home in college, commuting to Cleveland State University by bus. Although he didn't know it, his wife was also living at home with her parents, commuting to the Cleveland Institute of Art to become a sculptor. She rode the bus to college too. You can see where this is going. One day when they were 18 they happened to be riding on the same bus. They saw each other over the packed seats, smiled in recognition, and have been inseparable for the past 40 years.

Although he couldn't have elucidated it when he was five, my brother KNEW that this girl was the person he was destined to spend the rest of his life with. As Billy Crystal says in *When Harry Met Sally*, when you know that you want to spend the rest of your life with someone, you want the rest of your life to start right now. I believe that for my brother, the future was determining his actions in kindergarten, on that bus to college, and for the past 40 years.

Love at first sight, properly understood, is retrocausal.

Evolutionary Psychology

I used to teach Evolutionary Psychology as a routine part of my rotation of courses, but gave it up nearly a decade ago. It's become too political of a theory to teach to undergraduates. This is because it goes against the Standard Social Science Model (SSSM) that states that culture determines the boundaries of "hot-button" issues like gender, power, and sexuality. Evolutionary psychology (EP), on the other hand, argues that these issues are predominantly determined biologically. To put it simply, to teach from the SSSM is to teach from the *Left*; to teach EP is to teach from the *Right*. In higher education, it's safer to teach from the Left.

That's not to say that either of these approaches is correct or incorrect. In many ways evolution, when applied to psychology, is just a series of Rudyard Kipling's *Just So Stories*, like "How the Elephant Got Its Trunk." This is to say that you start in the present, go back in time to what is referred to as "the environment of evolutionary adaptedness," and propose a causal relationship between the past and the present. For example, researchers have found that women prefer taller men. No real surprise, yet there is a big difference between the sexes in terms of how great the height differential should be. Men prefer partners who are a little smaller than they are (3 inches on average) where women prefer partners who are much taller than they are (8 inches on average). Why? Evolutionary psychology would say that "sexual selection" (meaning the adaptiveness of certain characteristics) helps increase an organism's chances of attracting a mate and successfully reproducing. In the far past (that "environment of evolutionary adaptiveness"), taller men would be more likely to be able to defend women and their children from attack by other males. So modern women don't just prefer men who are a little taller than they are; they prefer men who are MUCH taller, even though we now have guns and police departments to protect us, and so height has become unrelated to the ability to defend loved ones. But that's the attraction of evolutionary psychology: the present is predicted from the past. One might ask why men would prefer women who are only a little smaller than they are, and EP provides a ready answer - taller women produce taller offspring. Why waste your resources on a much smaller woman when a taller woman produces children who will also be tall, and therefore desirable to future mates?

Sticking with height for another example, it is also thought to confer authority in men. After all, George Washington (at 6'2") towered over his colonial troops (who averaged 5'8"). In fact, it has been 120 years since the United States has elected a president who was shorter than the average American male of their time, and on average, presidents have been 4½ inches taller than the average male. For comparison, Barack Obama is 6'1" and Donald Trump is 6'3", so the trend doesn't seem to be changing. While this data is supportive of the evolutionary psychology position, the Standard Social Science Model is also able to explain the preference for taller men by relying on culture. The SSSM view is that people are acculturated in patriarchal societies which put a premium on men being tall. But what about Napoleon? He was 5'6" - average for his time and place.

So it's the past that determines the present? Not so fast. Evolution is as easily explained retrocausally. How? First, let's understand why evolution fails as a causal explanation. One of the problems with evolutionary theory is that the past determining the present doesn't work mathematically. Since the vast majority of random genetic mutations would lead to catastrophic results, and we have some idea of the rate of mutation in a particular time period, there just isn't enough time (even when we're talking about tens of millions of years) for *positive* random genetic mutations to occur. So how do we get Darwin's finches with different beaks depending on the food source of the island they live on? David Berlinski has pointed out (most recently in his book *The Deniable Darwin*) that rather than random mutation, evolution seems to have a guiding endpoint. It's a small step to suggest that the "endpoint" is working backwards in time retrocausally.

How about an example? While evolutionary theory is able to come up with an explanation for why taller men are preferable, the advent of blue eyes has been more of a problem. The fact is that 10,000 years ago, no humans had blue eyes; now, 17% of humans have blue eyes. Why? While Hans Eiberg from the University of Copenhagen lead the research team that determined that all people with blue eyes are descended from a single common ancestor who lived between 6,000-10,000 years ago, he sees no particular genetic advantage of the mutation from brown to blue eyes, and believes it to be no different from mutations for hair color, baldness, and beauty spots.

The problem with this belief is twofold. First, to go from one person to over a billion people with the same recessive gene mutation in a few thousand years means that people really, **really**, **REALLY** sought out blue-eyed mates to reproduce with. The evolutionary advantage of blue (or "lighter") colored eyes has been calculated at 3% per generation, an advantage equivalent to the development of articulate speech. And this occurred in an "environment of evolutionary adaptedness" - in other words, in a time before mass media and culture could "control" what people find attractive (according to the SSSM).

The second problem is that blue eyes are one of the only physical characteristics that is seen as desirable in both sexes. This is odd, as most physical characteristics are sex-typed like height (attractive in men, less attractive in women) or the evolutionarily all-important waist-to-hip ratio (attractive in women, meaningless in men). As an aside, so much research has been published on waist-to-hip ratios and fertility in women that it's pretty much canon in EP. Women with lower waist-to-hip ratios are healthier, have an easier time becoming pregnant, and are able to do so at earlier ages than women with higher waist-to-hip ratios. The waist-to-hip ratio also fluctuates slightly during the menstrual cycle, hitting the lowest point during ovulation, which is, again, when a woman is most fertile.

At this point you might be asking what the evolutionary explanation is for the preference for blue eyes? The answer is simple. There is none. This is a question which has thoroughly bamboozled geneticists and evolutionary psychologists. One proposed theory is that people with blue eyes are "easier to read" emotionally because others can subconsciously gauge their interest level through pupil dilation. This argument has not been tested (and was proposed by an undergraduate), but is congruent with the belief that people with dark irises are more "mysterious" and harder to "read."

There is a retrocausal explanation for blue eyes, and it's similar to another characteristic that is seen as attractive in both sexes: symmetry. People are not perfectly symmetrical, either in their faces or their bodies, and handedness (most people are right-handed) is an example of a directional asymmetry. Research has shown that animals who are symmetrical are healthier, have higher survival rates, and are more likely to reproduce. This is because asymmetries are usually caused by malnutrition, disease, or parasitic infection during development. In people, facial symmetry is seen as attractive, but not as attractive as a face which is *mostly* symmetrical, with some naturally occurring asymmetries. For example, Marilyn Monroe was almost always photographed from her right side - her "best" side.

However, I'm not proposing that blue eyes are a natural asymmetry that is seen as attractive. On the contrary, I propose that in the future everyone will have blue (or lighter) eyes - a retrocausal effect. Blue eyes are a "guiding endpoint" of evolution in the same way as articulate speech or facial symmetry. Remember, darker eye color is the dominant gene, and so it's evolutionarily a big deal for the blue-eyed recessive gene to be expressed in so many people in so short a time period.

Everyone can't have blue eyes, or even seek a mate who has them, but everyone can cosmetically change their eye color, and millions of people do.

Colored contact lenses which change brown or green eyes to blue (or about any other color, including red) have been available for over a decade, and millions of people choose to wear them. Is this due to media and fashion magazines which tell us that "blue is beautiful?" Remember, *that* media wasn't available to our ancestors.

The retrocausal explanation is clear - people in the present want to look like people in the future. And those people have blue eyes.

Luck

Many years ago, when I was in college, my friend Maddog and I went over to my friend Tom's house to pick him up for some adventure. Tom lived with his parents, who were avid lottery players. While waiting for Tom to get ready, Maddog and I made small talk with Tom's dad, but we could tell that the tension in the house was building because the daily "Pick 3" number draw was only minutes away. Tom came into the room with his mother, and she asked what the winning number for that day was. Maddog turned to her and nonchalantly said "184." Thirty seconds later they did the "Pick 3" drawing on television and it came up "184." Everyone shrieked, and Tom's mom asked Maddog what the "Pick 3" number would be tomorrow. We all had a laugh at that and then went out for the evening.

How had Maddog picked the right number? Did he "see" 30 seconds into the future? Was he just lucky? After all, probabilistically, he had a 1 in 1,000 chance of getting it right. Who knows?

About half of Americans play the lottery, and that added up to $71 billion in sales in 2017 (the most recent year for which numbers are available). That's significantly more than the $56 billion spent each year to attend sporting events, but is only half as much as the amount spent on gambling on the outcomes of those same sporting events (estimated to be $150 billion, with only $5 billion of that bet "legally").

But how do people pick their lottery numbers? Do they allow fate to decide, or do they attempt to achieve some control over their future winnings by picking their own numbers? Thankfully, there's an answer to both of these questions. About 70% of people allow the lottery machine to pick their numbers for them - they put their fate in the hands of perceived "randomness." Everyone else has their own strategies, most of which are not very original - birthdays, anniversaries, and other "lucky" numbers.

Patterns do emerge in the numbers that people pick. For example, the most common "Pick 3" numbers chosen by lottery players are 111, 222, 333, 777, and 999. Similarly, the most common "Pick 4" combinations are 1111, 2222, and 3333. It doesn't seem to occur to most lottery players that others are using their exact same strategy (a point that we will return to shortly). On June 21, 2019, the North Carolina lottery had 5,600 winners when 111 came up as the "Pick 3" number of the day. Just two days later, the North Carolina lottery had to pay out a record $7.8 million in prizes (to 2,000 winners) when the "Pick 4" came up as 0000. Willie Ward, who was one of the winners, said that he always plays zeros in both the "Pick 3" and the "Pick 4" games. "I love the zeros" Willie said. "I'm dedicated to them." The previous record was $7.5 million in 2012, when the "Pick 4" number was 1111. Finally, the next week (June 28, 2019), the North Carolina "Pick 3" winner came up as 000. It was not reported whether Willie Ward was a winner again, but it was a rough week for the North Carolina state lottery.

Airline disasters also seem to have a draw for lottery players. Perhaps most famously, on the first anniversary of the 9/11 attacks (so September 11, 2002) the New York state lottery "Pick 3" number came up as 911. Each of the 5,631 people who had played that number received $500 in winnings.

The New Jersey "Pick 3" lottery has both an afternoon and evening number draw, so people can play the lottery twice per day. On November 12, 2001, American Airlines Flight 587 crashed in Queens immediately after take-off. The "Pick 3" winner that night was 587. Even more oddly, the afternoon draw had been 578.

One last airline example, because it's a happy outcome. On January 15, 2009, Chelsey B. "Sully" Sullenberger landed his Airbus A320 in the middle of the Hudson River. The flight number? US Airways Flight 1549. The New York state lottery limits the number of people who can play a certain number on any given day (to control the damage from a mass payout), and had to suspend the number 1549 the next day. The actual "Pick 4" number that was drawn that day? 1548.

It's one thing to play airline flight numbers, but lottery officials also grow concerned when a large number of people play a seemingly random series of numbers and hit the jackpot. For example, the Powerball draw on March 30, 2005 had only one jackpot winner ($13.8 million) but 110 people who correctly picked 5 of the 6 numbers. To put it in perspective, Powerball would usually expect to pay out only five second place prizes (with a payout between $100k and $500k). Further complicating the situation was that the 110 winners all played the same numbers (22, 28, 32, 33, 39, and 40) and thus the SAME INCORRECT number (42 was the drawn Powerball number, not 40). Strangely, the 110 winners were spread across 29 states! Lottery officials suspected foul play and investigated. What they found was that everyone picked their numbers from the same place - a fortune cookie produced by Wonton Foods of Long Island. Ironically, the winning Powerball ticket had the numbers chosen randomly.

All of the previous examples rely on superstition, but what about science? Can probability theory be used to pick winning lottery numbers? Some have tried. For example, Matthew Vea, an Ernst & Young's financial services consultant, went through the MegaMillions numbers for over 4 years to find the numbers that came up most often. His results? The numbers 14, 36, and 48 come up far more often than they should (about 11.5% of the time), while 6, 47, and 49 are drawn the least often (about 6% of the time). That sounds scientific until you find out that other researchers, working from earlier data sets of MegaMillions draws, have come up with entirely different numbers, proving that it's difficult to predict probabilistically independent events, and basically a waste of time.

All of these examples, based on superstition or science, have the same thing in common, which is that they rely on the same causal mechanism - that the past will predict the future. Sometimes, based on probability, this leads to winning lottery numbers. These events are so unusual that they get written up in newspapers. But has anyone ever used the future to determine winning lottery numbers? Of course they have! And they've won.

Robert Uomini had a doctorate in Mathematics from UC Berkeley, but in 1995 he was selling computer advertisements for $25 apiece. He played the lottery for pure entertainment value and for the fantasy of buying a Lamborghini or a house in the south of France. He would usually go with the lottery machine "quick picks," but after looking them over, felt that they weren't random enough, and decided to generate his own numbers. But how? Theta waves!

The human brain generates four different types of waves which differ in amplitude and frequency: alpha waves, beta waves, delta waves, and theta waves. Without going too deep into the science, each of the waves generally corresponds with the activity people are engaged in, so relaxation or meditation are associated with alpha waves, interacting with others is associated with beta waves, and sleep is associated with delta waves. Theta waves are the most interesting for purposes of this discussion, as they are associated with daydreaming and creativity. Theta waves are often expressed when engaged in activities that don't require much mental concentration and allow the mind to wander. This is why many creative ideas come to people while in the shower, driving on the highway, out on a long run, or even when brushing their hair.

Robert Uomini decided to generate his lottery numbers while his theta brainwave was dominant, because research has tied theta rhythms to mental activities such as learning, memory, and navigation. He says that he got the lottery form and "just went into this theta thing."

All of a sudden, it felt like I was in the back of a train
in a tunnel and everything was racing away from me. I
had this funny depth perception. Numbers started
coming into my head. I didn't think about the numbers,
I just wrote them down. Then I used the same ticket for
two and a half years. And then I won.

Robert Uomini won $22 million with the numbers that had come to
him - 10, 19, 22, 26, 29, and 33. He didn't buy a Lamborghini or a house in the
south of France because the bottom of the Lamborghini would scrape on his
driveway, and he decided that he didn't want to leave the house where he had
raised his children. His only two splurges were diamond earrings for his wife
and $1 million to endow a Chair in the math department at UC Berkeley. In
the end, he said "it's sheer stupidity to play the lottery."

I believe that Robert Uomini won the lottery through a retrocausal
effect. While everyone else uses events which have already occurred (birthdays,
anniversaries, plane crashes) to generate their lottery numbers, Robert tapped
his theta brainwaves and opened his mind to the future. It wasn't an exact
science - he was able to see the sequence of numbers that would win, but not
when they would be drawn. So he played the same numbers until they hit. And
they did. And it made him a multimillionaire.

Luck, properly understood, is a retrocausal phenomenon.

Depression, and what it means to be human

In the past decade, psychology has become increasingly interested in time travel. Not the kind where you step into a machine and travel to the past or future, but something like it. Think about what you did yesterday. Maybe you went out to dinner in a restaurant. Where did you go? What did you have? Who was with you? Or think about your plans for this week. What's on your schedule? Where are you going to be? Who will you be there with? Humans have a unique ability to think about the past and plan for the future which sets them apart from the rest of the animal kingdom. This is a process known as *mental time travel* or MTT.

Consider our human ancestors tracking a buffalo on the savannah. They were able to differentiate the hoof of a buffalo from that of an antelope or a zebra. They were also able to tell how "fresh" the print was, whether the buffalo was alone or part of a group, and whether it was healthy or injured. The hunter had to rely on their past experiences to recognize what animal the tracks belonged to and foresee (or as the literature puts it, "pre-live") a future of where the buffalo is going. Even without distance weapons like a bow or a spear, the buffalo could be killed by running it to exhaustion and bludgeoning it to death. Contrast this with the way that lions hunt their prey. A lion will walk right over the tracks of an animal without noticing them. They lack the ability to associate the hoofprint with the prey they are seeking. Instead, lions stalk their prey. They see them, sneak as close as they can, and then charge in order to pounce or knock the animal over. It's the "smash and grab" approach to hunting, and works because most of the prey animals are faster than the lion. This is also why female lions often work together when hunting. But it's very different from the way that humans hunt. Humans are able to hunt the buffalo without ever *seeing* the buffalo. They know where it has been, and can follow where it is going. Seeing the buffalo after tracking it lets the hunter know that they were correct. This ability to think in terms of the abstraction of "past" and "future" is crucial and determines whether everyone eats or goes hungry. Unlike our animal brethren, we are not trapped in an "eternal present," but can readily recall the past and make plans for the future.

The ability to achieve mental time travel has its disadvantages too. In thinking of the past, we can see how things might have gone differently, a process that cognitive psychologists refer to as the *mutability of events*. For example, let's say that there are multiple ways for you to drive home from a grocery store, but you have a preferred way to return home that goes down

Main Street. On a particular day, the weather is nice and so you decide to drive home through a parkway which is shaded by trees. Suddenly, a deer shoots out of the woods and you strike it, killing the deer and "totalling" your car. While you're grateful to be uninjured, with time you begin to think about the accident and how things might have gone differently. What if you had gone shopping on a different day? What if you had gone shopping earlier in the day? What if you had just stuck to your usual drive home down Main Street?! Any of these alternatives would have prevented the accident. The mutability of events allows us to see how things would have gone differently if other, "better" choices had been made. This then leads to blame for the accident. If you had just driven down Main Street then nothing bad would have happened, so at some level, the accident was your fault. This is a tactic used all the time by defense attorneys to blame victims in court cases - "If you had not been walking through the park that night you wouldn't have been robbed. Therefore, don't you bear some of the blame for the robbery?"

Taking the mutability of events a step further is when people develop a focus on negative events from their past, an activity known as *rumination*. Think of all the things that have gone wrong in your life and the things that you might have said or done but didn't. All the injustices, indignities, and cruelty you have suffered. Now imagine thinking about them all the time. That's rumination. As you might expect, rumination leads to a gloomy outlook on people, relationships, and life in general, and is a major component in developing, prolonging, and intensifying depression. Ruminators are more likely to hold on to grudges and drive friends and family members away. In terms of gender differences, studies have shown that women report higher rates of depression, and it's often attributed to their disposition to rumination.

Part of the attractiveness of rumination as an explanation of depression is the causal link between the past and the present, and psychologists going back to Freud believed that past experiences and traumas determined present problems. But what about the other side of mental time travel? What about plans for the future?

Researchers have conducted studies where they randomly ping people throughout the day to ask about their thoughts and mood. They find that people are three times more likely to be thinking about the future than the past, and when they are thinking about the past, it is as a guide to what they should do in the future. These researchers believe that it is the "future focus" of people which determines their mental health. Martin Seligman, one of the founders of the positive psychology movement, goes as far as to say that instead of being called *Homo sapiens* ("wise man"), humans should be referred to as *Homo prospectus*, because plans for the future tend to dominate our thinking.

People who don't have depression report higher levels of happiness and lower levels of stress when thinking about the future and making plans. Having a "future focus" makes upcoming events seem more controllable and leads to greater *self-efficacy*, or confidence in our ability to create positive outcomes through our behavior. People with depression, on the other hand, tend to have a distorted view of their future, over-predicting failure and rejection from loved ones. These findings have led to an alternative view, where it is not traumas from the past, but an unrealistic and negative view of the future which leads to depression. The technical term for this is *dysfunctional prospection*, and it has three components. First, depressed people think about negative future scenarios, including images of their own death. This is particularly dangerous, as it correlates with a greater risk of suicide. Second, depressed people expect bad things to happen in the future, and feel that there is nothing they can do to stop them. This leads to a sense of hopelessness. Finally, depressed people believe that future bad things will happen due to their own faults and shortcomings. So according to this view, depression is not caused by rumination over the past, but rather a hopeless view of the future. Ironically, the mental time travel that distinguishes us as human and allows us to plan for the future leads to depression.

While conventional explanations of depression may focus on ruminations on the past or hopelessness about the future, a retrocausal explanation relies on the concept of *depressive realism*. Initially developed by Lauren Alloy and Lyn Abramson in 1979, depressive realism describes a consistent finding in psychological studies of people with depression - they judge their control of events more accurately than people who are not depressed. Rather than treating depressed people as if they have distorted views of the past and future, this theory argues that people with depression are far more realistic about their fate and their future. After all, life is a series of heartaches, suffering, and indignities which ends in death. To not be depressed about this state of affairs is to be unrealistically optimistic.

Let's revisit the idea of self-efficacy. People are asked whether they would classify themselves, in general, as "masters of their fate" who make the decisions which impact their lives, or "leaves in the wind" who react to events as they occur, but without much control over them. While "masters of their fate" are more psychologically healthy, it is the "leaves in the wind" who are more realistic about life. We can plan for the future and feel like we exert control over situations, but while people are injured and killed in auto accidents every day, no one puts "Get in auto accident" in their daily planner. To be psychologically healthy is to be confident, overly optimistic, and full of self-deception.

I will close with an example from research on intimate relationships. People with depression also tend to be high in the personality trait of *negative affectivity*, which means that they tend to dwell on their own faults and negative qualities, as well as those of their romantic partners, and really everyone else too. Not surprisingly, people high in negative affectivity are particularly vulnerable to failed intimate relationships. After all, it is difficult enough to be in a relationship with someone who is depressed, but who wants to be with someone who constantly criticizes them and points out their faults? Depression is not creating a distorted view of the future, but a realistic one. Due to retrocausality, people with depression are aware of a future where their relationships end badly and they are sad and alone. Who would be happy with that knowledge?

That is why depression, properly understood, is a retrocausal phenomenon.

Learning

One of the reasons why I still drive a car with a manual transmission is that I can park it with the keys in the ignition and don't have to worry about anyone trying to steal it. Not that anyone would want to steal a 1998 BMW Z3 convertible (a quintessential "old man's car" in 2020), but would a joy-riding teenager even know how to drive a manual transmission? While somewhere between 18 and 60 percent of Americans say that they can drive a manual, in my experience, "can" means "as long as I can stall it out every 20 feet." While they're still popular in Europe (and much of the developing world), only 2% of all cars sold in the United States in 2018 had a manual shifter, and the future seems to belong to "one-pedal" electric and autonomous vehicles.

As driving manual transmission cars goes the same way as candle making, it raises the question of how learning occurs, both intentionally and incidentally, and whether "learning" is yet another psychological activity that has a retrocausal explanation. I want to talk about some early research with cats in puzzle boxes and rats in mazes, and then give some examples from human research. We'll cycle back to driving cars too!

The crucial foundational research on learning and problem solving in animals was done by Edward Thorndike in 1898 as part of his dissertation research at Columbia University. He was interested in what he called *connectionism*, which posited that learning was based on the connections which were made between "situations" and "responses." He got the idea from the philosophical principle of "association," but instead of talking about how ideas become associated in the mind, Thorndike was interested in finding connections between objectively verifiable situations and the responses which were learned from them. In order to study these connections, he thought he needed to place animals into unique situations that they had to get out of by a particular response or series of responses. This is how he got the idea of putting cats into "puzzle boxes" (which were actually modified fruit crates). Each of the "puzzle boxes" had a unique "combination" of responses that the cat had to perform in order to escape and eat some food which was outside of the box (the reward for their escape). Of course, the situation was unique for the cat, and so they didn't KNOW what responses they had to do to get out, such as whacking at a string suspended from the top of the box or pushing at a pedal that was in the box with them. Each box had a new and unique "combination" and so the cats had to use trial and error (or in Thordike's phrasing, "trial and accidental success") in order to escape and eat the tasty treat. So, the first time the cat escaped, it was based on completely random behavior, but Thorndike found that in subsequent trials, the cats quickly produced the correct responses to escape the "puzzle box" they had been placed in. Thorndike believed that the correct responses were "stamped in" and the incorrect responses were "stamped out," and this was an objective behavioral way to show how learning occurred. He generalized these findings to create his *law of effect*, which posited that behaviors which were followed by positive outcomes were more likely to reoccur, and behaviors which lead to negative (or no) outcomes would stop. If this sounds suspiciously like B. F. Skinner's later theory of operant conditioning, it's because it is! Skinner would add the concept of reinforcement (both positive and negative) and the law of acquisition, but we don't need to get into that.

Thorndike's contemporaries saw the flaws in his research, and the Gestalt psychologist Wolfgang Kohler remarked that the cats could *only* use trial and error to initially escape the puzzle boxes, and if all learning required trial and error, then very little learning would occur. Kohler proposed that he (and everyone else) learned to problem solve through *insight* and used the story of Archimedes and the crown to make his point. If you're unfamiliar with the story, Heiro of Syracuse was presented with a golden crown by his goldsmith, but suspected that it wasn't made entirely of gold, so he gave it to Archimedes and told him to find out whether it was pure gold *without* melting it down or damaging it. This presented a real problem for Archimedes, so he decided to take a bath and think about it. As he sank down into the water, he realized that the water rose - his irregular volume displaced the water. He shouted "Eureka!" ("I've found it!") and in his joy, supposedly ran naked through the streets of Syracuse. His insight was that he could weigh the crown and see how much water it displaced, and then compare that to the same weight in gold, and the amount of water IT displaced. No trial and error, but rather an "ah ha!" experience. Kohler also added the idea of *incubation* to problem solving, which says that if you can't figure out how to solve a problem, walk away from it and let your "subconscious" work out the solution, which will come to you as a thrilling insight. I believe that Kohler was inadvertently proposing a retrocausal explanation of insight, and that "incubation" is actually tapping into knowledge of the future. Kohler wasn't just philosophizing about problem solving, and performed a series of studies with chimpanzees that showed that they were capable of problem solving through insight too, and published his research in *The Mentality of Apes*.

Thorndike also had critics within his own school of Behaviorism. Edwin Ray Guthrie criticized the "puzzle box" research within the context of his theory of "temporal contiguity" - that learning occurred only when two things were brought together in time. For Guthrie, one of the problems with Thorndike's research was that when the cat made the proper responses, they were immediately allowed to escape from the puzzle box. If there had been a five minute time delay between the proper response and the cat's escape, the cat would have never made the correct association between their behavior and its consequences, and no learning would have occurred. Therefore, temporal contiguity determines learning. Guthrie's other problem with Thorndike's research was that the food outside the box acted as a reward to "stamp in" the correct response. For Guthrie, there was no reason to consider the food to be a reinforcer that caused learning; instead, the food acted to prevent "unlearning" the association between the behavior and the escape. While this may seem to be philosophical word-play (because it is), it anticipates Tolman's research on learning, to which we now turn.

One of the key aspects of Thorndike's research, as mentioned by Guthrie, was that learning could not occur without a reward. This led Edward Tolman to investigate whether learning could occur without a reward through what he called *latent learning*. His study was ingenious, involved running rats in mazes, and leads to a retrocausal explanation of learning. The rats were put into two groups. The first group ran the maze and always found a reward for successfully arriving at the "goal box," meaning that they had successfully learned the maze. The "errors" that they made in running the maze (wrong turns, hesitations, etc.) as well as the time it took them to run the maze was recorded. Tolman found that over a series of trials, both the number of mistakes and the time it took to successfully make it to the goal box declined to the point where eventually, the rats ran the maze without any errors. The second group had no reward in the goal box for the first 20 trials that they were in the maze. They were just kept in the maze for a standard amount of time equivalent to how long it took the first group to run the maze. Suddenly, on the 21st trial, there was a reward in the goal box. According to Thorndike, since there had been no reward for the first 20 trials, no learning should have taken place, but Tolman found that the learning curve for the rats in the second group was MUCH steeper than for the first group. His interpretation was that the rats had learned the layout of the maze (represented in the mind as a "cognitive map") even without a reward, and only when food was present in the goal box did they demonstrate a "latent" learning of the maze. A retrocausal explanation would be more like the following: the rats were eventually going to learn the maze, and their experience of the maze without reward provided the context for that future knowledge to be deployed once they started getting a reward. So latent learning is really an artifact of retrocausal knowledge.

While the animal testing is interesting, I'd like to conclude this section with my own experience with learning material in psychology, as I believe it is a personal example of how human learning and cognition is impacted retrocausally. I was not a very good college student, but I've been a successful college professor in that I'm a tenured full professor who has taught 15 different courses in psychology. I took a lot of courses as an undergraduate (usually 17-20 hours every semester) and until my senior year was a psychology/history/Russian triple-major. However, if you just look at my grade point average (which was a 3.1), it doesn't seem like I was trying very hard. And you would be correct because I wasn't! I would make my college girlfriend nuts because I would never check my grade on a test. I would tell her that I did as well as I could, and that grades didn't really matter anyway. I didn't view high grades as a "reward" for learning. Psychology was my "main" major, and I didn't have an "A" in any psych classes during my sophomore and junior years. I attended class, but spent most of the lectures reading something else. Russian was my weakest major, and I earned a "D" in my final Russian language class. My knowledge of Russian today is abysmal, and I'm much more fluent in the French that I learned in high school. Yet I still love both history and psychology, and read extensively in both fields. It is said that you don't really understand something until you teach it to others, and I believe that my breadth of knowledge in psychology has retrocausally determined my college experience. How was a horrible student able to make it through an undergraduate career and succeed in graduate school? By knowing the material cold IN THE FUTURE! After teaching 15 different courses in psychology, my breadth of knowledge is pretty extensive. Certainly enough to get through an undergraduate program without really trying. I believe that the learning I did in college could be best described as latent learning - I was in the classroom but I wasn't paying much attention. It was my ability to tap into future knowledge that got me through college.

To bring us back around to cars, in the same way that only a few people still know how to crank-start a Model T Ford, in the future, no one will know how to drive a manual transmission. Or probably any car. The ability or need to physically interact with any machine is dwindling even in our own lifetimes.

Learning, properly understood, is a retrocausal phenomenon.

Intelligence

Are people getting smarter? Your answer to that question might depend on how much you have to drive as a part of your daily commute. Or whether you work in the service industry. Or whether you see the movie *Idiocracy* as a documentary. But it is an issue in intelligence testing. The controversy over what intelligence tests are measuring and what it means to do well on them has raged since Alfred Binet and Theodore Simon constructed the first tests for Parisian schoolchildren in the early 1900s. An issue which has not been discussed is the thesis that intelligence is a retrocausal phenomenon.

The early studies of intelligence were designed to determine which children needed extra help in school. Binet and Simon's goal was to identify a child's *mental level*, or how they compared to their age peers on a number of cognitive tasks. If a child scored low on their scales, they would be put into special remedial classes with greater individual attention and instruction. They believed that mental level, as measured by their tests, could be raised. They rejected the idea of *mental age*, a term introduced by German psychologist William Stern in 1911, because it led to the idea of an intelligence quotient (the ratio of mental age to chronological age x 100), which they considered to be misleading and potentially even dangerous. Their opposition didn't matter - IQ was too easy of a concept to understand and we still use it as shorthand for intelligence today. For example, the average adult IQ is 100, and a 130+ would indicate that a person is "gifted," where a 70 or lower would be classified as "borderline impaired or delayed." Binet died young (in 1911), but Simon was still opposed to the idea of IQ when he was interviewed at age 86 in 1973, saying that IQ was "a betrayal of the scale's objectives."

Intelligence testing is what put psychology on the map and made it pay. During World War I, the Army Alpha and Beta tests were created in order to determine which recruits would benefit from further training and instruction, but it was after the war that intelligence testing really took off. Since it was children who were primarily tested, one of the questions researchers had was whether children who had high IQ scores would end up "burning out" as they got older. It was the theory of "early ripe, early rot" and under extreme conditions, could lead to cases like Leopold and Loeb, two brilliant, wealthy college students in the 1920s who planned the "perfect crime" - kidnapping and murdering a 14-year-old. They believed that their "intellectual superiority" would allow them to get away with it, but of course they were caught and went to prison, even though they had Clarence Darrow as their defense attorney.

Lewis Terman decided to do a longitudinal study of intelligence starting in 1921. He was at Stanford, and had revised and restandardized the Binet-Simon scales to create the Stanford-Binet IQ test in 1916 (he would do a second revision in 1937), so he was very familiar with the issues in intelligence testing. He started with a pool of 250,000 children, all who were given the Stanford-Binet. The minimum criteria for inclusion in the longitudinal study was an IQ of 135 or above, and 857 boys and 671 girls were chosen for the study. Their average IQ was 151 (with a range between 135 and 200), and the average age of the children was 11. At the outset, commonalities in the childrens' backgrounds were assessed, and it was found that these children were typically early readers (by age 3 or 4) who had subsequently read widely in a number of topic areas. As a question that we will return to, are children who are early readers destined to be highly intelligent, or are highly intelligent people likely to be early readers? Retrocausality would argue for the latter explanation.

Terman was able to continue the study until he died in 1956, and other researchers have now continued it for eight decades. A problem with longitudinal studies is that people often drop out or the researchers lose touch with them; however, at the time of Terman's death, 95% of the "gifted children" were still participating in the research. So what did Terman find? First, none of the children became murderers or criminal masterminds, to put that stereotype away. At the time of the second follow-up, when the "Termanites" were in their late 20s, 87% of the men and 83% of the women had been to college (in a time when only 8% of the population were college graduates). At the time of Terman's last follow-up, the "children" were now middle-aged adults with successful careers and marriages. Most of the men (87%) held professional jobs (doctors, lawyers, teachers, etc.) and oddly for the era, 42% of the women worked full-time. A subsequent follow-up in the 1970's found that the lifetime divorce, suicide, and mental health problems of the "Termanites" were well below the national average. Terman and his colleagues were able to show that smart children did not "rot," but became "prudent and persistent" adults.

The retrocausal question remains though. Are intelligent people born that way, or is it their future educational attainment and careers that drives their intelligence? Of course, the answer might be neither, and this is where things get even *more* complicated. It turns out that people ARE getting smarter (at least on intelligence tests), a phenomena called the *Flynn effect*. Without going too deep into the weeds, it can be said that intelligence tests are updated and revised from time to time. For example, the Wechsler Intelligence Scale for Children (or WISC) was created in 1949, but updated to the WISC-R ("R" for "Revised") in 1971, the WISC-III in 1991, the WISC-IV in 2003, and the WISC-V in 2014. Flynn's initial work in the 1980s was to give children the current and earlier version of the same test. He found that children scored much better on the earlier test (the WISC) than they did on the (then) current version of the test (the WISC-R). Similarly, adults who had averaged a 103.8 IQ score on the Wechsler Adult Intelligence Scale-Revised (WAIS-R) averaged a 111.3 on the older version of the test (the WAIS). Subsequent research with larger samples and other intelligence tests have found the same phenomena, and show that IQ scores are increasing by about three points per decade. That's the Flynn effect.

This has led to a real conundrum because the tests were standardized on the people of their time. This would mean that if the average children of today (IQ=100) were to take the Stanford-Binet test from 1932, their average IQ would be a 126! More shockingly, a child from 1932 taking the SB5 (the 5th revision of the Stanford-Binet, released in 2003) would have an average IQ of 74, putting them in the category of "borderline impaired or delayed." What is going on here?! Were people in the past just dumber? Or are people getting smarter? Or is there a problem with the tests?

Several explanations of the Flynn effect have been proposed. First, maybe nutrition is better now, and that is leading to higher test scores? After all, people have gained about a centimeter of height per decade for the past hundred years. Perhaps that's tracking with intelligence? This would argue that we're much smarter than our grandparents. A second explanation involves child-rearing practices. People in the past didn't have parenting books like the *What to Expect* series or Dr. Spock's *Baby and Child Care* (now in the 10th edition). A third explanation involves infectious diseases. Perhaps the eradication of parasitic infection and the prevalence of diseases like malaria explain increasing IQs? The problem with this explanation is that malaria was eradicated from the United States in 1951, but scores keep going up. A fourth explanation involves schooling and test-taking ability. Maybe universal education has made children both smarter and more sophisticated in their understanding of how to take tests? While education does have an impact on IQ scores, the United States has had universal high school public education since the 1930s, so this explanation is unlikely. A fifth explanation is basically "all of the above." While each of the previous explanations can be dismissed, all of them in combination might provide a picture of what is happening.

I believe that the two most compelling non-retrocausality arguments come from James Flynn himself, and cognitive scientist Ulric Neisser. Flynn proposes that based on interviews with uneducated peasants in rural Russia in 1900, people in the past thought more "concretely" than people do today. If you asked the Russian peasant what a crow had in common with a fish, they would say "absolutely nothing." After all, you can't eat a crow, but you can eat a fish, and a crow can peck at a fish, but a fish can't do anything to a crow. If you told them that they were both animals, they would say "No, one is a bird, and the other is a fish." Flynn believes that this concrete thinking leads to problems with classification and taking hypothetical situations seriously. He points out that in 1900, only 3% of jobs were "cognitively demanding," but now 35% of jobs meet that criteria. He leaves unanswered the question of whether 65% of Americans today would think that a crow has nothing in common with a fish. I believe that Flynn's explanation would be more compelling if most Americans had the same education and life experience as an uneducated peasant in rural Russia in 1900.

Although he admits that there is little "direct evidence" for his explanation, Neisser believes that the Flynn effect can be explained through increased exposure to visual media. He writes that "from pictures on the wall to movies to television to video games to computers, each successive generation has been exposed to far richer optical displays than the one before" and this has created a *visual analysis* form of intelligence. According to Neisser, the Flynn effect is resolved because people today really are "smarter" in a particular way than their great-grandparents were. However, I think the major problem with Neisser's explanation is that it implies that children who spend a lot of time playing video games (an activity unavailable to our ancestors) should have higher IQ scores than children who spend a lot of time reading (an activity readily available to our ancestors). And yet they don't.

It's obvious to me that the explanation for the Flynn effect is retrocausal. First, consider the Terman longitudinal research. Children who scored well on the Stanford-Binet were likely to be early readers who went on to college and the "cognitively demanding" careers that Flynn believes are important. This thinking is *causal*: smart kids do well on IQ tests and go on to have careers that require intelligence. But the *retrocausal* explanation makes more sense: people who will have "cognitively demanding" jobs later in their life are early readers who do well on IQ tests. It's the future "cognitive demands" that determine the early intelligence, not the other way around. To return to Flynn's example of the uneducated rural Russian peasant in 1900, they wouldn't have to be intelligent to work on a collective farm in the 1920s, so they weren't very intelligent in 1900. Their future, unfortunately, determined their past.

Flynn is correct that jobs are increasingly becoming more "cognitively demanding" through the impact of technology. Low skill (meaning "not cognitively demanding") jobs are increasingly automated or replaced by robots. This is a trend which is accelerating. And consider the UT-1 Ultra Trencher! It weighs 60 tons, drops to the ocean floor, and digs trenches for oil pipelines and telecommunications cables. We've gone from people who dig ditches (like the Russian peasant from 1900), to people on machines who dig ditches, to people who remotely control 60 ton robots that dig ditches under the ocean floor. Even ditch-digging is becoming a "cognitively demanding" occupation. This means that people are doing better on intelligence tests because their future jobs require them to be more intelligent, regardless of the work they do.

Intelligence, properly understood, is a retrocausal phenomenon.

Death

It seems fitting to end this book with death, because if someone is alive, death is guaranteed to be in their future, and this is, after all, a book about how the future impacts the present and past. The problem is in determining whether death is having any identifiable retrocausal impact. In theory, if one is of a religious bent, we could talk to the non-divine people that Jesus is recorded to have raised from the dead: Lazarus and the daughter of Jarius. The problem is that they lived two thousand years ago. While they might still be walking the earth (there are no extant death certificates for either of them), this brings us into the area of religion rather than science.

Let's stay within science. Luckily, there is an entire field of research which examines near-death experiences (NDEs) with journal articles, books, and research conferences. While this is not technically "death" (it's "near-death" or "death-adjacent"), it's also not very scientific. For example, a common experience of someone undergoing an NDE is floating outside of the body. A famous case of this involved a migrant woman named Maria who was admitted to a hospital in Seattle in 1977 while in cardiac arrest. After being resuscitated by her doctors, she described a tennis shoe that was on a window ledge on the third floor of the hospital that she had noticed while floating around. Sure enough, when someone went to look, there was a tennis shoe outside the window exactly as Maria had described it. How did the shoe get there? How did she see it? Who knows? But it's an intriguing event.

So how would a scientist study this "floating" phenomenon? The AWARE (AWAreness during REsuscitation) study asked this exact question, and came up with a unique solution. Since a common source of NDEs is cardiac arrest, what if pictures were placed on a high ledge in rooms where cardiac patients were resuscitated? The pictures are only visible to someone who is floating near the ceiling of the room, and the hospital staff doesn't know what the picture is either. Presumably, patients would float to the top of the room, see the picture, and be able to describe it to the researchers later. The study's lead researcher, Dr. Sam Parnia, got 15 hospitals in the US, the UK, and Austria to participate. Over 4 years and 2,060 cardiac arrests, they only found two patients who were resuscitated and reported experiencing floating as a part of their NDE. One of the patients subsequently died, but the other (a 57-year-old man) was able to accurately describe the doctors who were defibrillating him. Unfortunately for the researchers, the patient was defibrillated in a room that did not have a ledge with a picture on it. No one said this research was going to be easy.

Other researchers have sought to interview people who have had NDEs, people known in the NDE community as "experiencers." This type of research is by far the most common, with over 600 articles based on interviews with 3,500 "experiencers" as of 2020. However, many aspects of this research are problematic. First is the self-selection bias of people who have had NDEs. About a quarter of "experiencers" report having a frightening or unpleasant near-death experience, and they might be less likely to come forward and be interviewed for a research project. A second problem is with the researchers themselves. Many have a religious bias and are seeking proof of life after death by studying NDEs. For example, Raymond Moody's book *Life After Life* came out in 1975 and pretty much set the NDE narrative of floating down a tunnel towards a bright light, and then seeing dead relatives. Moody interviewed 100 "experiencers" for the book, and has inspired a number of others to write books with titles like *Proof of Heaven*, *Imagine Heaven*, and *Heaven is for Real*. The final problem in this research is that it is based on peoples' memory of past events, what therapists would call retrospective data. Most of the interviews are conducted years after the NDE has taken place, and memory is not a video camera, so people construct a story which encompases what they remember, what they were told happened (after all, they were clinically dead), and perhaps, what they *wish* had happened. The personal narrative of their near-death experience is, at best, unreliable.

While the idea of a soul leaving a physical body is congruent with Christian theology, near-death experiences have been found to be similar across different cultures and different religions. This similarity in experience has led some researchers away from cultural and religious interpretations of NDEs, to instead focus on the brain as a neurobiological mechanism that changes as it approaches death. But how does it change? And how can this change be studied? After all, hooking people in cardiac arrest up to brain scanning equipment in order to obtain data to test an NDE hypothesis is impractical and likely unethical. So we have to work with the data we have, and the data we have is thousands of interviews with people who have had NDEs.

Maybe an NDE is just an altered state of consciousness which is similar to other altered states? Perhaps certain drugs can induce an NDE-like experience? In an ingenious study from 2019, researchers performed a linguistic analysis of NDE interviews to determine how they were similar to the experiences of people doing various drugs. Their dataset allowed them to compare 625 NDE narratives to over 15,000 "drug experience" narratives with 165 psychoactive substances, and the findings were revealing. Two drugs stood out above the rest - ketamine and DMT. Ketamine was first synthesized in 1962 as an anesthetic, but has recently been used as a treatment for anxiety and depression. It is used by some people recreationally (and is known as "Special K") because at low doses it can induce hallucinations and an out-of-body experience. DMT (technically, *N,N*-Dimethyltryptamine) is a hallucinogen which can produce the feeling of floating and an out-of-body experience. Both drugs are popular because they're fast acting (within minutes) and the "trip" is short (typically 30-60 minutes) in comparison to a hallucinogen like LSD, which can take over an hour to kick in for a "trip" that can last 15 hours. Both drugs can also produce a frightening and disorientating experience, just like an NDE. While ketamine is synthetic, DMT may be present in trace amounts in the brain, and DMT enthusiasts claim that it is primarily released at birth, in dreams, and at death. These qualities make DMT a prime candidate for explaining why NDEs are similar across humanity - we're all carrying the "drug" to induce an NDE with us all the time, and it is released when the brain is dying, like during a cardiac arrest. By this point you might be asking how any of this research is related to retrocausality. And it isn't. The research discussed thus far is attempting to explain NDEs. In order to understand the retrocausality of death, we need to examine the death process as recorded in research on hospice patients.

Unlike people undergoing the acute terror of cardiac arrest, people in hospice know that they are dying. They've already been released from a hospital and are transitioning from emotional and physical suffering to the acceptance of their imminent death. Their experiences are not "one-time" encounters with death like NDEs, but rather a process of end-of-life dreams and visions (ELDVs) which they describe as "more real than real." And their ELDVs are retrocausal.

A few statistics to begin. A little over 88% of hospice patients report having at least one ELDV, usually visits from friends or relatives who have already passed on, bringing messages of forgiveness and love. For 99% of patients who experience an ELDV, it feels as real as anything else they've experienced in their life. For example, Frank, a former steelworker, complained to his doctor that he was having trouble sleeping because "it's been great to see my Uncle Harry, but I wish he would shut up!" Of course, Uncle Harry had been dead for 46 years. And he still wouldn't shut up.

An interesting way that ELDVs are different from NDEs is that they are a recurrent phenomena that tracks with the health of the person having them. For example, a patient who enjoyed dreaming of dead friends they hadn't seen in years experienced a temporary improvement in their health, and the dreams stopped. Their assessment of the situation was "I'm back to reality. I miss the other stuff." People who work in hospices come to realize that when the ELDVs return, death soon follows.

Another interesting aspect of ELDVs is that they blend into the person's awake state, so that a common reaction is "Why am I seeing this? Am I going crazy?" A patient who was having recurring dreams of two dead aunts standing by her bed watching over her became alarmed when she began seeing them while awake too. She was also concerned because as an intensely religious person, she expected to see angels by her bedside, not dead aunts! Evidence such as this argues strongly against the ELDVs being generated by what researchers call *demand characteristics*, or people just seeing what they want to see.

Hospice patients don't just dream about dead people; family and friends who are still alive are also present. However, researchers have found that as the patients get nearer to death, the ELDVs increase in frequency, and the content of the ELDVs feature more and more dead people. In the words of hospice physician and researcher Christopher Kerr, "It appears that dreams of the deceased hold prognostic significance based on changes in frequency and content as the end draws near."

By this point, you might be wondering how ELDVs are proof that death is retrocausal. The answer is simple, and merely requires a change in perspective. Hospice patients who experience ELDVs believe they're being visited by people from their past who have died. In actuality, the dead visitors are from the patient's *future*. And usually their very near future.

William Faulkner said that "The past is never dead. It's not even past." Hospice patients show us that at the end of life, people from our past guide us from our future.

Death, properly understood, is retrocausal.

Select References

Memory

Baruss, I., & Rabier, V. (2014). Failure to replicate retrocausal recall. *Psychology of Consciousness: Theory, Research, and Practice, 1*(1), 82-91.

Bem, D. J. (2011). Feeling the future: Experimental evidence for anomalous retroactive influences on cognition and affect. *Journal of Personality and Social Psychology, 100*(3), 407-425.

Bem, D. J., Tressoldi, P., Rabeyron, T., & Duggan, M. (2015). Feeling the future: A meta-analysis of 90 experiments on the anomalous anticipation of random future events. *F1000 Research, 4,* 1188. https://doi.org/10.12688/f1000research.7177.2

Galak, J., LeBoeuf, R. A., Nelson, L. D., & Simmons, J. P. (2012). Correcting the past: Failures to replicate psi. *Journal of Personality and Social Psychology, 103*(6), 933-948.

Mossbridge, J. A., & Radin, D. (2018). Precognition as a form of prospection: A review of the evidence. *Psychology of Consciousness: Theory, Research, and Practice, 5*(1), 78-93.

Ritchie, S. J., Wiseman, R., French, C. C. (2012). Failing the future: Three unsuccessful attempts to replicate Bem's 'Retroactive Facilitation of Recall' effect. *PLoS ONE, 7*(3): e33423. https://doi.org/10.1371/journal.pone.0033423

Robinson, E. (2011). Not feeling the future: A failed replication of retroactive facilitation of memory recall. *Journal of the Society for Psychical Research, 75*(904), 142-147.

Schwarzkopf, D. S. (2018). On the plausibility of scientific hypotheses: Commentary on Mossbridge and Radin (2018). *Psychology of Consciousness: Theory, Research, and Practice, 5*(1), 94-97..

Love

Anderson, L. (2015, April 8). *The Rules, 20 years later.* Vox, https://www.vox.com/2015/4/8/8353915/rules-dating-advice

Chung, N. (2013). *An existential-phenomenological investigation of unrequited love at first sight.* [Unpublished doctoral dissertation]. California Institute of Integral Studies.

Fein, E., & Schneider, S. (1995). *The Rules: Time-Tested Secrets for Capturing the Heart of Mr. Right.* Grand Central Publishing.

Fellizar, K. (2019, June 3). *Is love at first sight real?* Bustle. https://www.bustle.com/p/is-love-at-first-sight-real-5-signs-its-happening-to-you-6746694

Grant-Jacob, J. A. (2016). Love at first sight. *Frontiers in Psychology, 7,* 1113. https://doi.org/10.3389/fpsyg.2016.01113

Harrison, M. A., & Shortall, J. C. (2010). Women and men in love: Who really feels it and says it first? *The Journal of Social Psychology, 151*(6), 727-726. https://doi.org/10.1080/00224545.2010.522626

Naumann, E. (2004). *Love at first sight: The stories and science behind instant attraction.* Sourcebooks Casablanca.

Reiner, R. (Director). (1989). *When Harry Met Sally* [Film]. Castle Rock Entertainment.

Swami, V. (2011). Love at first sight? Individual differences and the psychology of initial romantic attraction. In T. Chamorro-Premuzic, S. von Stumm, & A. Furnham *The Wiley-Blackwell handbooks of personality and individual differences* (pp. 747-772). Wiley-Blackwell.

Zsok, F., Haucke, M., de Wit, C., & Barelds, D. (2017). What kind of love is love at first sight? An empirical investigation. *Personal Relationships, 24*(4), 869-885. https://doi.org/10.1111/pere.12218

Evolutionary Psychology

Berlinski, D. (2010). *The deniable Darwin and other essays.* Discovery Institute Press.

Eiberg, H., Troelsen, J., Nielsen, M., Mikkelsen, A., Mengel-From, J., Kjaer, K. W., Hansen, L. (2008). Blue eye color in humans may be caused by a perfectly associated founder mutation in a regulatory element located with the HERC2 gene inhibiting OCA2 expression. *Human Genetics, 123*(2), 177. http://doi.org/dqsx5d

Etcoff, N. (1999). *Survival of the prettiest: The science of beauty.* Doubleday.

Hoover Institution. (2019, July 22). *Mathematical challenges to Darwin's theory of evolution.* [Video]. YouTube. https://www.youtube.com/watch?v=noj4phMT9OE&list=LL1bfd7pctj2XFHEbhRThcGQ&index=5&t=0s

Judge, T. A. (2018). *Does height make right? U.S. presidents and their height, weight, and greatness.* The Ohio State University. https://fisher.osu.edu/blogs/leadreadtoday/blog/does-height-make-right-u-s-presidents-and-their-height-weight-and-greatness/

Miller, A. S. & Kanazawa, S. (2007). *Why beautiful people have more daughters: From dating, shopping, and praying to going to war and becoming a billionaire - two evolutionary psychologists explain why we do what we do.* Perigee Trade.

Singh, D. (1993). Adaptive significance of waist-to-hip ratio and female physical attractiveness. *Journal of Personality and Social Psychology, 65*, 293-307.

Singh, D. & Luis, S. (1995). Ethnic and gender consensus for the effect of waist-to-hip ratio on judgments of women's attractiveness. *Human Nature, 6*, 51-65.

Stulp, G., Buunk, A. P., & Pollet, T. V. (2013). Women want taller men more than men want shorter women. *Personality and Individual Differences, 54*(8), 877-883.

Stulp, G., Buunk, A. P., Verhulst, S., & Pollet, T. V. (2015). Human height is positively related to interpersonal dominance in dyadic interactions. *PloS One, 10*(2), e0117860.

Thornhill, R. & Moller, A. P. (1997). Developmental stability, disease, and medicine. *Biological Reviews of the Cambridge Philosophical Society, 72*, 497-548.

University of Copenhagen. (2008, January 31). *Blue-eyed humans have a single, common ancestor.* ScienceDaily. https://www.sciencedaily.com/releases/2008/01/080130170343.htm

Luck

Blain, G. (2009, January 17). Lottery sales soar for lucky No. 1549. *New York Daily News.* https://www.nydailynews.com/new-york/lottery-sales-soar-lucky-no-1549-article 1.420762

Blitz, J. (Director). (2010). *Lucky* [Documentary Film]. Big Beach Films.

Doomed plane's number drawn in N.J. lottery. (2001, November 15). *The New York Times*. https://www.nytimes.com/2001/11/15/nyregion/doomed-planes-number-drawn-in-nj-lottery.html

Hamilton, B. (2010, January 24). Lottery's luckiest choices revealed. *New York Post*. https://nypost.com/2010/01/24/lotterys-luckiest-choices-revealed

Hasselmo, M. E. (2005). What is the function of hippocampal theta rhythm? Linking behavioral data to phasic properties of field potential and unit recording data. *Hippocampus, 15*(7), 936-949. https://doi.org/10.1002/hipo.20116

Herrmann, N. (1997, December 22). What is the function of the various brainwaves? *Scientific American*. https://www.scientificamerican.com/article/what-is-the-function-of-t-1997-12-22

Huddleston, T. (2019, June 25). *Over 2,000 people picked all zeros as their lottery numbers - now they're splitting a $7.8 million prize*. CNBC. https://www.cnbc.com/2019/06/25/over-2000-people-picked-all-zeros-as-lottery-numbers-and-won.html

KHOU 11. (2019, February 11). *The lottery numbers that get picked the most* [Video]. YouTube. https://www.youtube.com/watch?v=hQR1tz9cGH4

Leonhardt, M. (2019, December 12). *Americans spend over $1,000 a year on lotto tickets*. CNBC. https://www.cnbc.com/2019/12/12/americans-spend-over-1000-dollars-a-year-on-lotto-tickets.html

Mikkelson, D. (2006, September 25). *Did winning lottery numbers come from a fortune cookie?* Snopes. https://www.snopes.com/fact-check/fortune-cookie-fortune

Mikkelson, D. (2016, January 12). *Sept 11 lottery coincidence*. Snopes. https://www.snopes.com/fact-check/the-lottery/

O'Brien, S. (2017, September 11). *Americans spend $56 billion on sporting events*. CNBC. https://www.cnbc.com/2017/09/11/americans-spend-56-billion-on-sporting-events.html

Rubenstein, S. (1995, January 14). Skeptic wins $22 million in lottery he calls stupid. *San Francisco Chronicle*. https://www.sfgate.com/news/article/Skeptic-Wins-22-Million-In-Lottery-He-Calls-3048712.php

Sherman, A. (2019, April 17). *Legal gambling from your phone could be a $150 billion market, but making it happen will be tough*. CNBC. https://www.cnbc.com/2019/04/27/fanduel-draftkings-race-to-win-150-billion-sports-betting-market.html

Depression

Adelson, R. (2005). Probing the puzzling workings of depressive realism. *Monitor on Psychology, 36*(4), 30.

Alloy, A. B., & Abramson, L. Y. (1979). Judgement of contingency in depressed and nondepressed students: Sadder but wiser? *Journal of Experimental Psychology: General, 108*(4), 441-485.

Baumeister, R. (2016). Emotions: How the future feels (and could feel). In M. E. Seligman, P. Railton, R. F. Butler, & C. Sripada (Eds.), *Homo prospectus* (pp. 207-223). Oxford University Press.

Bucklin, S. (2017, June 22). *Depressed people see the world more realistically*. Vice. https://www.vice.com/en_us/article/8x9j3k/depressed-people-see-the-world-more-realistically

D'Argembeau, A. (2016). The role of personal goals in future-oriented mental time travel. In K. Michaelian, S. B. Klein, & K. K. Szpunar (Eds.), *Seeing the future: Theoretical perspectives on future-oriented mental time travel* (pp. 199-216). Oxford University Press.

Lavender, A., & Watkins, E. (2004). Rumination and future thinking in depression. The *British Journal of Clinical Psychology, 43*(2), 129-142. https://doi.org/10.1348/014466504323088015

Hoerl, C., & McCormack, T. (2016). Making decisions about the future: Regret and the cognitive function of episodic memory. In K. Michaelian, S. B. Klein, & K. K. Szpunar (Eds.), *Seeing the future: Theoretical perspectives on future-oriented mental time travel* (pp. 241-266). Oxford University Press.

Miller, D. T., & Gunasegaram, S. (1990). Temporal order and the perceived mutability of events: Implications for blame assignment. *Journal of Personality and Social Psychology, 59*(6), 1111–1118. https://doi.org/10.1037/0022-3514.59.6.1111

Moore, M. T., & Fresco, D. M. (2012). Depressive realism: A meta-analytic review. *Clinical Psychology Review, 32*(6), 496-509.

Papageorgio, C., & Wells, A. (2003). An empirical test of a clinical metacognitive model of rumination and depression. *Cognitive Therapy and Research, 27*, 261-273.

Pezzulo, G. (2016). The mechanisms and benefits of a future-oriented brain. In K. Michaelian, S. B. Klein, & K. K. Szpunar (Eds.), *Seeing the future: Theoretical perspectives on future-oriented mental time travel* (pp. 241-266). Oxford University Press.

Roberts, B. W., Kuncel, N. R., Shiner, R., Caspi, A., & Goldberg, L. R. (2007). The power of personality: The comparative validity of personality traits, socioeconomic status, and cognitive ability for predicting important life outcomes. *Perspectives on Psychological Science, 2*, 313-345.

Seligman, M. E., & Roepke, A. M. (2016). Prospection gone awry: Depression. In M. E. Seligman, P. Railton, R. F. Butler, & C. Sripada (Eds.), *Homo prospectus* (pp. 281-304). Oxford University Press.

Seligman, M. E., & Tierney, J. (2017, May 19). We aren't built to live in the moment. *The New York Times*. https://www.nytimes.com/2017/05/19/opinion/sunday/why-the-future-is-always-on-your-mind.html

Solomon, B. C., & Jackson, J. J. (2014). Why do personality traits predict divorce? Multiple pathways through satisfaction. *Journal of Personality and Social Psychology, 106*, 978-996.

Watson, D., & Clark, L. A. (1984). Negative affectivity: The disposition to experience aversive emotional states. *Psychological Bulletin, 96*(3), 465–490. https://doi.org/10.1037/0033-2909.96.3.465

Learning

Brown, T. K. (2014, June 4). *How do people lose their native language?* BBC. https://www.bbc.com/news/blogs-magazine-monitor-27690891

Evarts, E. C. (2016, September 27). *Why are manual transmissions disappearing?* U.S. News & World Report. https://cars.usnews.com/cars-trucks/best-cars-blog/2016/09/why-are-manual-transmissions-disappearing

Ferris, R. (2020, April 15). *Manual transmission cars are disappearing, but purists prefer to drive a stick shift.* CNBC. https://www.cnbc.com/2020/04/15/manual-transmission-cars-are-disappearing-but-purists-prefer-to-drive-a-stick-shift.html

Guthrie, E. R. (1935). *Psychology of Learning.* Harper.

Khazan, O. (2014, July 24). *Forgetting and remembering your first language.* The Atlantic. https://www.theatlantic.com/international/archive/2014/07/learning-forgetting-and-remembering-your-first-language/374906/

Kohler, W. (1925). *The Mentality of Apes.* Harcourt, Brace & World.

Thorndike, E. L. (1898). Animal intelligence: An experimental study of the associative processes in animals. *The Psychological Review: Monograph Supplements, 2*(4), i-109. https://doi.org/10.1037/h0092987

Tolman, E. C., & Honzik, C. H. (1930). Introduction and removal of reward, and maze performance in rats. *University of California Publications in Psychology, 4*, 257-275.

Tolman, E. C., Richie, B. F., & Kalish, D. (1946). Studies in spatial learning. I. Orientation and the short-cut. *Journal of Experimental Psychology, 36*(1), 13-24. https://doi.org/10.1037/h0053944

Intelligence

Acemaglu, D, & Restrepo, P. (2018). Low-skill and high skill automation. *Journal of Human Capital, 12*(2), 204-232.

Eppig, C., Fincher, C. L., & Thornhill, R. (2010). Parasite prevalence and the worldwide distribution of cognitive ability. *Proceedings. Biological Sciences, 277*(1701), 3801-3808. https://doi.org/10.1098/rspb.2010.0973

Flynn, J. R. (1984). The mean IQ of Americans: Massive gains 1932 to 1978. *Psychological Bulletin, 95*(1), 29-51. https://doi.org/10.1037/0033-2909.95.1.29

Flynn, J. R. (1987). Massive IQ gains in 14 nations: What IQ tests really measure. *Psychological Bulletin, 101*(2), 171-191. https://doi.org/10.1037/0033-2909.101.2.171

Flynn, J. R. (2009). *What is Intelligence?* Cambridge University Press.

Flynn, J. R. (1998). IQ gains over time: Toward finding the causes. In U. Neisser (Ed.), *The rising curve: Long-term gains in IQ and related measures* (pp. 25-66), American Psychological Association. https://doi.org/10.1037/10270-001

Friedman, H. S., & Martin, L. R. (2012). *The Longevity Project: Surprising discoveries for health and long life from the landmark eight decade study.* Plume.

Kern, M. L. & Friedman, M. L. (2008). Early educational milestones as predictors of lifelong academic achievement, midlife adjustment, and longevity. *Journal of Applied Developmental Psychology, 30*(4), 419-430. https://doi.org/10.1016/j.appdev.2008.12.025

Mone, G. (2008, April 3). *Massive underwater ditch-digging robot.* Popular Science. https://www.popsci.com/scitech/article/2008-04/massive-underwater-ditch-digging-robot

Neisser, U. (1997). Rising scores on intelligence tests. *American Scientist, 85*(5), 440-447.

Rindermann, H., Becker, D., & Coyle, T. R. (2017). Survey of expert opinion on intelligence: The FLynn effect and the future of intelligence. *Personality and Individual Differences, 106*, 242-247. https://doi.org/10.1016/j.paid.2016.10.061

Ritchie, S. J., Bates, T. C., & Plomin, R. (2015). Does learning to read improve intelligence? A longitudinal multivariate analysis in identical twins from age 7 to 16. *Child Development, 86*(1), 23-36. https://doi.org/10.1111/cdev.12272

Sears, R. M. (1977). Sources of life satisfactions of the Terman gifted men. *American Psychologist, 32*(2), 119-128. https://doi.org/10.1037//0003-066x.32.2.119

Sears, P. S., & Barbee (1977). Career and life satisfactions among Terman's gifted women. In J. C. Stanley, W. C. George, & C. H. Solano (Eds.), *The gifted and the creative: A fifty-year perspective* (pp. 28-65). Johns Hopkins University Press.

TED. (2013, September 26). *James Flynn: Why our IQ scores are higher than our grandparents'* [Video]. YouTube. https://www.youtube.com/watch?v=9vpqilhW9uI

Terman, L. M. (1926). *Genetic studies of genius: Vol. 1. Mental and physical traits of a thousand gifted children.* Stanford University Press.

Terman, L. M., & Oden, M. H. (1947). *Genetic studies of genius: Vol. 4. The gifted child grows up.* Stanford University Press.

Terman, L. M., & Oden, M. H. (1959). *Genetic studies of genius: Vol. 5. The gifted group at mid-life.* Stanford University Press.

Wolf, T. H. (1973). *Alfred Binet.* University of Chicago Press.

Death

Alexander, E. (2012). *Proof of Heaven: A neurosurgeon's journey into the afterlife.* Simon & Schuster.

Bryant, B. (2018, September 14). *A DMT trip "feels like dying" - and scientists now agree.* BBC. https://www.bbc.co.uk/bbcthree/article/dd52796e-5935-414e-af0c-de9686d02afa

Burke, J. (2015). *Imagine Heaven: Near-death experiences, God's promises, and the exhilarating future which awaits you.* Baker Books.

Burpo, T., & Vincent, L. (2010). *Heaven is for real: A little boy's astounding story of his trip to Heaven and back.* Thomas Nelson.

French, C. C. (2001). Dying to know the truth: Visions of a dying brain, or false memories? *The Lancet, 358*(9298), 2010-2011.

Grant, P. C., Depner, R. M., Levy, K., LaFever, S. M., Tenzek, K. E., Wright, S. T., & Kerr, C. W. (2020). Family caregiver perspectives on end-of-life dreams and visions during bereavement: A mixed methods approach. *Journal of Palliative Medicine, 23*(1), 48-53.

Hoffman, J. (2016, February 2). *A new vision for dreams of the dying.* The New York Times. https://www.nytimes.com/2016/02/02/health/dreams-dying-deathbed-interpretation-delirium.html

Kerr, C. W. (2020). *Death is but a dream: Finding hope and meaning at life's end.* Avery.

Kerr, C. W., Donnelly, J. P., Wright, B. A., Kuszczak, S. M., Banas, A., Grant, P. C., & Luczkiewicz, D. L. (2014). End-of-life dreams and visions: A longitudinal study of hospice patients' experiences. *Journal of Palliative Medicine, 17*(3), 296-303.

Koch, C. (2020, June 1). *What near-death experiences reveal about the brain.* Scientific American. https://www.scientificamerican.com/article/what-near-death-experiences-reveal-about-the-brain

Levy, K., Grant, P. C., & Kerr, C. W. (2020, January 24). End-of-life dreams and visions in pediatric patients: A case study. *Journal of Palliative Medicine,* ahead of print, https://doi.org/10.1089/jpm.2019.0547

Lichfield, G. (2015, August). *The science of near-death experiences.* The Atlantic. https://www.theatlantic.com/magazine/archive/2015/04/the-science-of-near-death-experiences/386231

Martial, C., Cassol, H., Charland-Verville, V., Pallavicini, C., Sanz, C. Zamberlan, F., . . . & Tagliazucci, E. (2019). Neurochemical models of near-death experiences: A large-scale study based on the semantic similarity of written reports. *Consciousness and Cognition, 69,* 52-69.

Martone, R. (2019, September 10). *New clues found in understanding near-death experiences.* Scientific American. https://www.scientificamerican.com/article/new-clues-found-in-understanding-near-death-experiences

Moody, R. (1975). *Life after life.* Mockingbird Books.

Nour Foundation. (n.d.). *The AWARE study.* https://www.nourfoundation.com/events/Beyond-the-Mind-Body-Problem/The-Human-Consciousness-Project/the-AWARE-study.html

Parnia, S., Spearpoint, K., de Vos, G., Fenwick, P., Goldberg, D., Yang, J, . . . & Schoenfield, E. (2014). AWARE - AWAreness during REsuscitation - A prospective study. *Resuscitation, 85*(12), 1799-1805.

Taub, B. (2017, July 5). *Do our brains produce DMT, and if so, why?* Beckley Foundation. https://beckleyfoundation.org/2017/07/05/do-our-brains-produce-dmt-and-if-so-why/

TED. (2015, December 2). *Dr. Christopher Kerr: I see dead people: Dreams and visions of the dying* [Video]. YouTube. https://www.youtube.com/watch?v=rbnBe-vXGQM

van Lommel, P., van Wees, R., Meyers, V., & Elfferich, I. (2001). Near-death experience in survivors of cardiac arrest: A prospective study in the Netherlands. *The Lancet, 358*(9298), 2039-2045.

Zarley, D. B. (2020, January 2). *Ketamine explained: Understanding the Special K drug.* Freethink. https://www.freethink.com/articles/special-k-drug-ketamine

48

One more thing . . .

I value your feedback on this book and your thoughts on retrocausality. As a college professor, I am used to the feedback of student evaluations at the end of every semester, and can appreciate both the positive and negative comments. So send me an email to let me know your thoughts. I'm easy to find online - I'm the Mark Hatala who is a college professor, and not the one who is a dentist or the golf pro.

If you enjoyed this book and found it thought-provoking, I would appreciate you leaving positive feedback in whatever venue you choose. Your experience will help others make a decision on whether to choose this book.

I will close by saying that I believe everyone has things that they can teach in this life, and most things are learned outside of any classroom. I put lots of YouTube videos up about the topics that interest me and the classes I teach, so mostly videos on writing, romantic relationships, retrocausality, and time travel. The opportunity to teach people I will never have the chance to have in a physical classroom means a lot to me, and so does your reading this book. Thank you!

Printed in Great Britain
by Amazon

23156724Π00030